D0463174

ANTEUS

MONSTERS OF MYTHOLOGY

25 VOLUMES

Hellenic

Amycus
Anteus
The Calydonian Boar
Cerberus
Chimaera
The Cyclopes
The Dragon of Boeotia
The Furies
Geryon
Harpalyce
Hecate
The Hydra
Ladon
Medusa
The Minotaur
The Nemean Lion
Procrustes
Scylla and Charybdis
The Sirens
The Spear-birds
The Sphinx

Norse

Fafnir
Fenris

Celtic

Drabne of Dole
Pig's Ploughman

MONSTERS OF MYTHOLOGY

ANTEUS

Bernard Evslin

CHELSEA HOUSE PUBLISHERS

New York   Philadelphia

1988

EDITOR
Remmel Nunn

ART DIRECTOR
Giannella Garrett

PICTURE RESEARCHER
Susan Quist

DESIGNER
Victoria Tomaselli

EDITORIAL ASSISTANT
Nicole Bowen

CREATIVE DIRECTOR
Harold Steinberg

3 5 7 9 8 6 4

Library of Congress Cataloging-in-Publication Data

Evslin, Bernard.
Anteus.

(Monsters of mythology)
Summary: Recounts the myth of the giant son of
Mother Earth who, with his bodyguards, Gobi,
Mordo, and Kell, battled Hercules.
1. Mythology, Greek. [1. Mythology, Greek] I. Title.
II. Series: Evslin, Bernard. Monsters of mythology.
BL785.E97   1988   292′.13   87-24929

ISBN 1-55546-241-3

Printed in Singapore

For Cody Clinton,
our smallest giant

Characters

Monsters

Anteus (an TEE uhs)	A giant, son of Mother Earth
Gobi (GO bee)	Giant archer who serves Anteus
Mordo	Giant cudgeller who also serves Anteus
Kell	Third of the giants serving Anteus; a skillful butcher
Hecate (HECK uh tee)	Queen of the Harpies

Gods

Zeus (ZOOS)	King of the gods
Hera (HEE ruh)	Queen of the gods

Gaia
(GAY uh or JEE uh)
Mother Earth

Prometheus
(proh MEE thee uhs)
A Titan, friend to man

Mortals

Hercules
(HER ku leez)
Son of Zeus, strongest man in the world

Libyans
(LIB ih uhns)
Hordes of them

Amaleki
(uh MAL e ki)
Brave mountaineers

Others

Sharks, octopi, camels

Phoenix
(FEE nihx)
A bird who abides in flame and arises from the ashes, unconsumed

Contents

1

Cannibal Stew

The parched hump of land called Libya was very different in the first days. It wasn't dry; it was green and wet. In fact, *Libya* meant "rainfall," and that spur of Africa was one of the most fertile spots on earth. But its people were not happy, for they were ruled by a monster.

His name was Anteus. He was the youngest of those dread creatures planted in Mother Earth by the Serpent of Chaos. Half-brother to the gigantic one-eyed Cyclopes and to the Hundred-handed Giants, Anteus was a giant also, and the most brutal of all that brood.

Many years before, his fancy had been caught by rich green Libya. He had invaded it, and made himself king by destroying everyone who stood in his path. He rapidly enlarged his kingdom, for he exulted in battle. There was nothing he relished more than the crunch of bones and the smell of blood. The shrieks of the wounded and the rattling gasps of the dying were music to his large hairy ears. And in the short intervals of peace, he amused himself by tormenting his subjects.

His entire court was composed of giants. Courtiers, counsellors, and the officers and men of the Royal Guard were gigantic. When they all reveled, which they did nightly, the mountains rumbled, the earth shook. And when their song was borne on the wind, utter choking fear took those who heard it. For this was the song:

"The stew, the stew,
the cannibal stew!
All you've heard is true
about what
goes in that pot . . .

Not pork, or mutton,
or costly beef
but eyes and nose,
fingers and toes
of rebel or thief
or those doing time
for any crime . . .

Into the pot,
ready or not . . .
with pepper and garlic
onion and thyme . . .

To boil and simmer
until it's through . . .
the stew, the stew,
the cannibal stew!
Served from the pot,
piping hot . . .

The stew, the stew,
the cannibal stew!
Why feed prisoners,
who can feed you?"

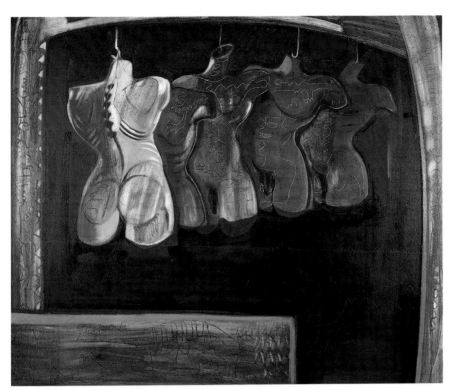

Into the pot . . . were thrown those who had
happened to offend the king . . . or, simply, certain
meaty-looking unfortunates who chanced to attract his notice.

Indeed, over a fire-pit dug into the courtyard, a huge iron pot seethed and bubbled. Into this pot, as the song said, were thrown those who had happened to offend the king in some way—or, simply, certain meaty-looking unfortunates who chanced to attract his notice.

And although there were many, many reasons to fear Anteus, who, in a temper, had been known to trample an entire village underfoot, this steaming iron pot became a special symbol of terror.

But the people of this unhappy land, like all folk everywhere, were unable to live without hope. And there was a prophecy abroad, which no one dared speak aloud, but was whispered

There was a prophecy abroad . . .
whispered from household to
household. It was: "Help will come from the sea."

from household to household. It was: "Help will come from the sea." Just six words, very short ones, but they fed the flickering flame of hope that warmed the Libyans through years of icy despair.

But like many other a tangled tale of monster and hero, the adventure that was to give meaning to this prophecy was being brewed in high, hidden councils. The fate of this monstrous king, youngest son of Mother Earth, was sprouting far from earth, out of plots woven by the feuding gods.

You might say it began with Prometheus.

2

Sport for the Gods

When Zeus first became king of the gods, there was a Titan named Prometheus who occupied a special place in the heavens. He dwelt alone in a cloud-castle, refusing to join the court or take sides in any quarrel.

He was so wise that everyone sought his counsel. Zeus alone disliked him, but was not ready to show his feelings.

Prometheus came to him one day and said: "You have just begun your reign and I have no wish to discourage you, but I must tell you that we gods are doomed."

"We are immortal," said Zeus.

"We cannot die in a gross physical sense," said the Titan. "But we can cease to be gods. And that for gods is worse than death."

"What threatens us?"

"We are being starved."

"What do you mean?"

"A god's nourishment is to be worshiped. But there is nobody to do that."

"We have each other," said Zeus.

"And we love or hate each other, or, mostly, are indifferent. But we cannot worship each other because we are all of the same family."

"Do you have a remedy, oh wise one, or have you come only to spread gloom?"

"I have a suggestion," said Prometheus. "I propose that we plant a new species in this garden of earth. And these new beings, created by us, resembling us in some ways, will lack our power, of course, but will have what we lack—the capacity to worship."

"To worship *us*, you mean?"

"Exactly."

"Your idea has some merit . . ."

"It is you, oh Zeus, they will especially worship."

"Me?"

"You are king of the gods. Of course they will worship you most."

"The idea gains merit even as you speak, good Titan. I shall consider it carefully."

Zeus decided to take the Titan's advice. After several trials, he succeeded in creating a clever two-legged race and set the first batch down on earth, dividing them into male and female so that they could begin to breed. At first, he spent hours watching them, but ceased to be amused by their antics. They seemed to be showing little impulse to worship their creator. . . . They did occasionally tie a bundle of straw into a kind of doll, mumbling to it and offering bits of food. But Zeus could not connect that crude figure with himself. So he lost interest.

The other gods, however, were fascinated—for a different reason. They began to believe that Zeus had planted mankind on earth as a landowner stocks a trout stream. Hunting humans became the gods' favorite pastime. It didn't provide the thrills of hunting a wild boar who could turn upon you with razor tusks, or a lion with claws that could rend you to shreds; man had neither horns nor tusks, nor claws, and was too slow-footed to offer the excitement of the chase. But the creature did possess that which other animals did not: self-consciousness, a sense of the future, a shuddering aversion to death and remarkable skill at evading it. Also, and most entertaining of all, these creatures were questioners; they groped for answers. Unlike other prey, they tried to understand what was happening to them. They could not comprehend the invisible arrows that struck out of nowhere, killing young and old, the strong and the feeble. And their agonized confusion amused the gods mightily. The anguished explanations humankind found for god-sport convulsed the

Prometheus, who had appointed himself protector of humankind, came to Zeus and said: "You who made man, why do you destroy him?"

Zeus summoned the gods to a grand conclave.

Olympians with laughter. Manhunting became a craze. And the herds were dwindling rapidly.

Prometheus, who had appointed himself protector of humankind, came to Zeus and said: "You who made man, why do you destroy him?"

"I'm not destroying him," said Zeus. "Oh, I bag one or two occasionally. But that's not destroying, that's *culling*. Improves the stock, you know. They breed quite rapidly."

"Not as rapidly as they're being killed. Look down, if you don't believe me. You'll see that your herds are shrinking daily."

"Perhaps. I hadn't really noticed."

"Please notice," said Prometheus.

"In regard for your age and reputed wisdom," said Zeus, "I have overlooked a certain lack of respect in your manner toward me. But I must warn you, my patience is not inexhaustible."

"If I have taken liberties, my lord, it is in your service. I promised you that if you created the race of man, he would nourish you with his worship. You are disappointed because he has not yet displayed that talent."

"Yes."

"But—and pardon me again, oh King—you have not waited long enough. The talent for worship, which is an offshoot of the capacity for wonder and the impulse toward praise, is something unique to mankind, and will develop only as he emerges from the animal state. Give him time, more time, I pray, and you will be pleased beyond measure."

"You are eloquent on this creature's behalf," said Zeus.

"It is on your own behalf, my lord. Stop the slaughter. Let him develop at his own rate. He will learn to rejoice in your handiwork, and sing your praises so beautifully that you will be entranced."

Thereupon, Zeus summoned the gods to a grand conclave. They thronged his throne room. He sat on the enormous throne made of cloud-crystal and congealed starfire, and wore his ceremonial sunset robes of purple and gold. The scepter he bore was a volt-blue zigzag shaft of lightning.

"Oh Pantheon," he thundered, "hear my words! Our herds are being slaughtered at a rate that approaches extermination. I have decided to be displeased by this, and hereby impose game laws. The monthly kill shall not exceed six per god. And I mean six adults, no children under twelve, no pregnant females or nursing mothers. . . . Severe penalties attach to transgression. Whoever exceeds his quota shall be shackled to the roots of a mountain in Tartarus and abide in suffocating darkness through eternity. I have spoken. You may go."

The new law was not popular. Hera came raging to Zeus one day, and although he was omnipotent, she was his wife and had one unique power; she could make him miserable. So he spoke to her gently and asked why she was so angry.

"It's that ridiculous law of yours," she hissed.

"You don't think the quota large enough? I didn't realize you were so keen a huntress, my queen."

"It's not that!" she shouted. "But I did fill my bag early this month, and now there's someone down there who needs killing."

"Wait till next month," said Zeus.

"I can't!"

"What's your hurry?"

"She's offended me."

"Something personal?"

"Very personal. I hate her. I must kill her now. Please, my lord."

"Very well, but don't make a habit of this sort of thing. We who make laws shouldn't break them."

Hera did not hear his last words. She was sliding down a sunray. And in a few minutes had cooled her wrath by murdering the unlucky girl who had offended her. . . . But what Zeus had feared came to pass. Other gods heard of this and came storming into the throne room, citing points of personal privilege and demanding that their quotas be raised.

Finally, Zeus became exasperated. The assembled gods saw that he was simmering with fury. He stamped his foot and the marble floor cracked. The blue lightning shaft that was his scepter went white-hot in his hand. Beyond the windows, thunder rolled. The gods shuddered. They knew that Zeus, generally good-natured, was sheer catastrophe when aroused, and that no one on heaven or earth would be safe from his wrath. They understood this because they knew the depths of their own cruelty, and he was of the same breed, but more powerful.

So they bowed their heads and did not respond when he tongue-lashed them, lowering the monthly kill-quota from six to four and laying a total ban on any complaint against the game laws. They filed out silently, submissively, and for a while were very careful about staying within their quotas.

But as time passed they worked out a way to break the law without getting punished. They used monsters.

Poseidon invented this method when a little village happened to displease him. A fishing village it was, beautifully set among hills rolling down to the sea. Only a handful of huts then, but it had been foretold that this little place was to become the most important city in the world. And since the people here drew their living out of the sea, Poseidon, master of the deep, expected them to name their village after him. But Athene, goddess of wisdom, had ideas about this village too. She meant to plant special people there and make it a place famous for wisdom.

Green robed, green bearded, Poseidon coasted in on a wave and strode toward the huts—immense, dripping, eyes full of stormy light. He spoke, and his voice was like the surf battering the cliffs.

"Good folk," he roared softly, "I am Poseidon, earthshaker, lord of the sea. It is I who have given you an ocean to harvest, taming the wild fathoms for your sake, stocking them with fat fish. Therefore, I ask, when you come to name this place, as soon you must, call it, please, after me, and I shall be your patron and protector forever."

He whistled up a great wave, which curled over him and drew him from the beach to the sea.

As soon as he had vanished, Athene appeared, shining so brightly in the dust of the little street that it hurt to look at her. She was clad in blue. An owl sat on her shoulder, and she bore spear and shield.

"Good folk," she said, and her voice was like the west wind making a harp of the trees, "I am Athene, daughter of Zeus, goddess of wisdom, and I am prepared to look upon you with great favor. Name this little village after me and you shall see it grow into the most worthy city in the world, home of sage and warrior, yes . . . and of a prophetess who will decipher the scroll of stars and read what is to come. These rude huts will grow into marble mansions; temples will gleam upon the hills, and thousands of years from now the very syllables of your name shall be a chime of glory. . . .

"I am Poseidon, earth-shaker, lord of the sea."

"And to prove my power, I give you this gift. Behold!"

She raised her spear high and stabbed it into the earth. It stood, quivering. Before the amazed eyes of the villagers, it began to sprout green branches. Fruit hung upon the boughs. Athene plucked a naked child from the street and lifted him so that he could reach into the tree. He snatched the fruit, stuffed his mouth, and gobbled happily. She kissed him and put him down.

"This tree is called the olive," she said. "Its fruit will feed you, and what is not used for food will be turned into wealth. For you will press the fruit of the olive, and its clear oil will be coveted by the tribes of earth and they will trade for it, sending you what is most precious to them—silks and amber, copper, spice, horses, slaves. And you shall grow rich and strong. All for giving your village my name."

The people fell on their knees and thanked the goddess, and named the village Athens. And the goddess departed.

All she had promised came true. But other things happened too.

For Poseidon was very angry. He took great pleasure in whipping up winds to sink the Athenian ships, sending great waves to wash away beaches and bury houses under tons of water, and drown the cattle in the fields.

Nor did all this satisfy him, for the Athenians were a stubborn tribe. They built their homes again, and built new boats, and launched them right into his sea to hunt for fish before the next storm hit.

So Poseidon called up a huge serpent from the depths. It was a hundred feet long and could swallow a fishing vessel in one gulp, nets and crew and all. . . . It appeared offshore one sunny afternoon and swallowed a whole little fleet. It devoured half the village before nightfall.

Poseidon trod the swell, capering and chortling as he watched the fleet being destroyed. The mighty jaws of the sea serpent gaped and crunched down on a vessel, crushing it between

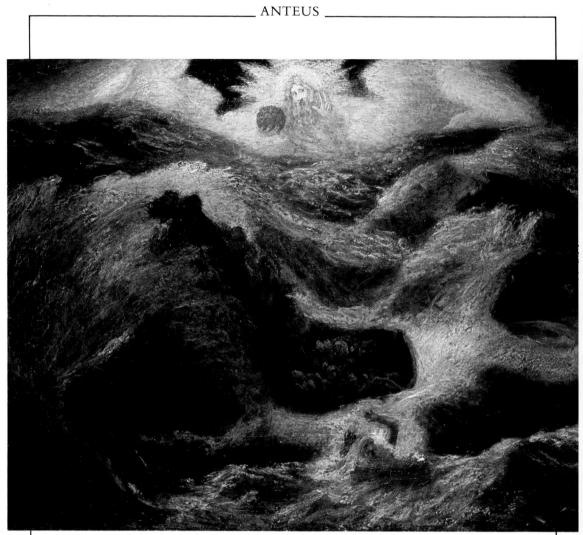

*Poseidon called up a huge serpent from the
depths. . . . It appeared offshore one sunny
afternoon and swallowed a whole little fleet.*

gigantic teeth. As the beast held one ship in his jaws, he smashed
another with his flailing tail. And the only reason there were any
Athenians left to rebuild their village was that Poseidon realized
he was using up his entire stock of this particular entertainment
in a single afternoon, and decided to save some for later. So he
called off his serpent, who swallowed a final fisherman and sank
to the bottom.

Now the other gods had observed Poseidon's vengeance and saw that it was a good idea to use monsters in that way. It allowed them to punish those they had taken a dislike to while still remaining within the law. Even Athene, who was furious at Poseidon for tormenting her favorite villagers, nevertheless called up monsters from time to time, and sent them to devour those who had offended her.

And the custom grew.

3

Gaia's Spell

he ancient earth-mother observed all this, and made certain plans.

"My youngest son, Anteus, is terrible in battle," she said to herself. "And will certainly be persuaded by one vengeful god or other to embroil himself in some dangerous feud. . . . Now, he's the most powerful of my offspring, the beautiful brute, and should be able to exterminate any pesky hero who dares challenge him. Nevertheless, I intend to take no chances with that precious life. . . . I shall concoct a spell that will assure him victory in all encounters."

Thereupon, she descended into the deepest cavern where an outlicking of the earth's core-fire smoldered in a natural stone basin. A spring of pure water ran through this basin and was kept at a boil. . . . This was Mother Earth's own cauldron where she brewed her most potent spells.

Muttering, she dropped herbs in the boiling water. As the steam wrapped her in a fragrant veil, she began to chant:

"Oh, you who decree
whatever must be,
I call to you
from my deepest core. . .

If my son, Anteus
is ever thrown,
let him touch earth
who gave him birth . . .

I shall staunch his gore,
his strength restore . . .
He shall rise from me,
as mighty as before . . ."

At this very moment, as it happened, Anteus was being threatened by an enemy more deadly than any he had ever met. They were the *Amaleki*, a warlike tribe of mountaineers—huge wild-bearded hot-eyed men; their women were just as big and just as fierce. This tribe had evolved a battle plan which always worked. During the short intervals of peace, they spent their time collecting the largest, roundest boulders they could find. These they lined up and balanced on a ridge at the top of the mountain. They had built this ridge strategically, laying logs in a trench to form a long mound just high enough to hold the great boulders teetering, emplaced against the mountain wind, but so balanced that a strong shove would send them thundering down the slope.

The boulders were always in place. When some were used in battle, the tribesmen would gather a fresh supply. Then, when an invading force approached, the Amaleki would send out a small patrol whose duty was not to fight, but to retreat. This force was made up of half-grown youths, boys and girls, who considered it the greatest honor to be able to risk their lives in this way. For it was dangerous duty. These youngsters were mounted on purebred racing camels, the most valued stock in all the northern rim of Africa.

*Muttering, Mother Earth dropped
herbs in the boiling water.*

The patrol would ride out to meet the enemy, allow itself
to be spotted, then turn tail and pretend to flee. The invaders
would immediately charge after them. The youths, expert riders
all, would pretend to be racing their camels at full stride; in reality,
they would be reining them in, traveling only at half-speed, al-
lowing the enemy to catch up . . . almost, not quite.

Retreating in this fashion, the patrol would lure the enemy
into the valley. When the invaders filled the pass, the mountaineers, stationed at both peaks, would launch their boulders.

Now, fate had decreed that Mother Earth's new spell was
to be tested at the very moment of its brewing. As Gaia, lodged
in her deepest cavern, was muttering over her cauldron, and the
magic vapors were steaming out of the cave—up, up, through
seams of coal and iron, through sapphire bed and fertile muck—

just at that moment, Anteus was racing ahead of his army, charging after the Amaleki patrol. . . . The white camels were running before him, carrying their young riders toward the mountain pass, but running as fast as they could; for Anteus could cover fifty yards at a stride and was gaining on them.

The patrol rode into the fatal valley, Anteus rushing after them. His giants were nowhere in sight; he had left them far behind. And the mountaineers, seeing the gigantic figure enter the trap, assumed that the rest of his army was on his heels, and began to roll their boulders.

A huge rock hit Anteus, knocking him off his feet. Other boulders rained down; rock fell on rock, chipping each other, filling the air with flying shale. Anteus was buried deep. And the mountaineers cheered as they saw the monster vanish under the rockfall.

They cheered too soon. For the first wisps of vapor from the magic cauldron drifted up through the valley bed and touched Anteus as the rocks fell. Dimly, he heard a voice chanting:

> ". . . let him touch earth
> who gave him birth . . .
> I shall staunch his gore,
> his strength restore . . .
> He shall rise from me,
> as mighty as before . . ."

The massive weight of rock had driven him to the floor of the valley, deep into the lap of his mother. Half crushed as he was, bones shattered, ripped open, bleeding from a hundred wounds, he touched the primal energy that had made him be. He drank of her strength. He felt a strange force surging through him. A marvelous elation sang through his veins . . . a joyous power.

He arose, shrugging off shale. He climbed to his feet, rocks cascading off his shoulders like water off a breaching whale. The

mountaineers, staring from above, were amazed to see the entire valley shudder. The enormous rock pile was heaving as though the earth were quaking beneath. Before their astounded gaze a giant arose, holding a boulder in each huge hand.

He hurled the boulders, first at one peak, then at the other, crushing dozens of the Amaleki with each throw. By this time, his own troops had arrived. He motioned them up one slope; he, himself, charged up the other. The brave mountaineers, who had never been defeated, streamed down to meet the giants.

They were massacred. Clubbed, stomped, hurled bodily off the mountain, or simply had their necks wrung like chickens. Some few were able to flee, and hide in caves. All the rest were slaughtered.

The giants were too heavy to ride camels. So they skinned the prize beasts like rabbits and roasted them over their campfires. Camel meat is tough and stringy, but the giants were very hungry.

From that day on, Anteus knew himself to be invincible. Earth's magic never failed. Stricken to the ground, he would rise again, stronger than before, and destroy whoever had felled him.

And it was this magical endowment that served him so well when he finally battled Hercules.

4

Bowman, Banger, Butcher

Anteus had picked giants for his Royal Guard—not simply outsized mortals but the offspring of monsters who had abducted nymphs and spawned gigantic, shaggy humanoid creatures. When he had recruited the largest and most savage of these, he trained them in the use of weapons. And although the weakest of them was capable of finishing off an armed warrior with his bare hands, they were kept hard at work until they were expert with bow, sword, spear, and battle-axe.

Now, Anteus was not the kind of war chief who stood on a hill well behind the front line, looking at maps. He led his men into battle. He charged like a bull, leaping over ditches, crashing through walls, battering to death anyone who couldn't scurry out of his way . . . leaving his men to mop up after him. Which meant cutting the throat of anyone left alive.

If the enemy were strong enough to field an army against him—which seldom happened—the Royal Guard dogged the king's footsteps as he rushed into the hottest part of the battle, forming a hedge of blades about him.

After leading his troops through several campaigns, and studying each man's performance, Anteus selected three of his Guardsmen as his personal escorts, who would accompany him everywhere, on and off the field, and might be called upon for special tasks. They were the three most ferocious fighters, of course; their names were Gobi, Mordo, and Kell.

Gobi was a bowman, but with too powerful a pull for any wooden bow. He had to make himself a special weapon. After a successful mammoth hunt, when a beast had been killed with the loss of only thirty beaters, Gobi claimed a tusk for himself. The slain animal had been exceptionally big, even for a mammoth—whose size is calculated as having been at least twice that of our own elephant—and its tusk was more than fifteen feet long.

Gobi split that tusk. And the shaft of ivory, cut and polished and bound at each tapered end with copper wire, became his bow. A cured strand of mammoth gut was his bowstring. His arrows, plumed with an eagle's tailfeathers and tipped with razor-sharp bronze points, were longer than ordinary spears.

When he bent that bow almost double and let his arrow fly, the enormous shaft could split an oak tree and pass through an armored man standing behind it.

Only Gobi himself could use that bow. Anteus was even stronger than Gobi and could bend it easily, but the bow was too refined a weapon for him; he preferred a club or his great mallet fists.

Mordo worshiped Anteus and copied everything he did. The club became his favorite weapon, and he had a collection of the most massive bludgeons ever used. Most of them were hardwood, carved to a perfect balance, but he also had one cudgel of glittering brass for ceremonial slaughter. And, in one battle, it was said, having shattered his club while squashing a chariot, he had raced to a nearby olive grove, uprooted a full-grown tree and used that as a club—roots, branches, and all—flailing an entire enemy patrol to bloody gobbets of flesh.

Modeling himself further on Anteus, Mordo sometimes cast aside his club and waded into battle armed only with his fists. He toughened his hands by soaking them in salt water. And when he clenched those huge paws into fists, planted his legs, thick as trees, and swung his oxbow shoulders, whipping his long arms about, then, indeed, those fists became weapons as deadly as any ever forged in a smithy.

As for Kell, he was a man of blades. He liked to cut and thrust. His dagger was as long as the usual sword, his sword longer than a lance. The shaft of his spear was tall as a mast. When he went into battle with these blades stabbing and slicing, he wrought such carnage that he chose to clothe himself not in armor but in a long one-piece leather apron such as butchers wear. Indeed, he was known as "the butcher," and was perhaps the most feared of Anteus's band of killers.

A young poet, once, made reckless by moonlight, composed a song and was foolish enough to sing it:

"Gobi, Mordo, Kell . . .
Bowman, Banger, Butcher,
Serve the tyrant well . . .
And though we go there first,
we'll wait for them in hell . . ."

He vanished very soon afterward and was never seen again. And although people remembered the song and sometimes whispered it to themselves, no one dared sing it aloud. Indeed, it wasn't heard again for many years—not until a young hero named Hercules landed on a Libyan beach and started doing what he had sworn to do.

5

Hera's Grudge

Hercules' second task had been to kill the hundred-headed Hydra—each of whose heads held fifty teeth, and whose bite was so poisonous that a single scratch from any one of those five thousand teeth would kill a hippo in the wink of an eye.

After Hercules had slain the Hydra, he dipped an arrow into its envenomed blood so that he might have one ultimate weapon. Then, afterward, he found that he was unable to make himself use that arrow no matter how great his peril. For he was afraid that if he did use it, its poison would enter the flowing waters, and be carried by the wind, and seep into the earth, poisoning crops and cattle—and people. He felt that he would rather lose his own life than do such a thing.

Nevertheless, he kept the poisoned arrow. And its very possession was to cause him endless woe—which began when he faced Anteus.

It happened this way:

Of all the females in the universe, human and divine, Hera, Queen of the Gods, was considered the most fortunate. Her wealth was as boundless as her extravagance. Her power was limited only by the will of her husband, Zeus, and not always then. And her majestic beauty was renewable by means of a magic spring in which no one else was permitted to bathe.

Nevertheless, for all her wealth and power and beauty, Hera was not happy.

Having made a habit of indulging every whim, she could be thrown into a tantrum by the slightest disappointment. And because she considered now that she was suffering a series of

For all her wealth and power and beauty, Hera was not happy.

major disappointments, her fury was shaking heaven and earth, and beginning to ruffle even the icy composure of the gods.

"I simply can't bear it," she snarled to herself. "That scurvy little lout, Hercules, has managed to defeat every monster I've thrown against him. It's beyond belief how he has been able to do this. But he has . . . he has. . . . He simply refuses to be vanquished, the mangy cur. And if I don't destroy him soon, I'll suffocate with rage. I'm finding it hard to breathe right now. The trouble with me is that I'm simply too kindly by nature to pursue a feud the way I should. What I need is some truly murderous counsel."

Whereupon, she sent for her friend, Hecate, Queen of the Harpies, and the world's foremost expert on various forms of vendetta and mayhem.

Upon receiving Hera's message, the young hag who was Hecate spread her great wings and flew from her underworld aerie up to the top of Mount Olympus, where dwelt the high gods. She found Hera in the orchard. Sunlight sifted through a lacework of branches, and the two towering females met in a play of checkered light and amid the mingled fragrance of crushed grass and ripening fruit.

"Esteemed mistress! Patroness!" cried Hecate. "Beloved friend. How can I serve you?"

"Good Hecate, teach me to kill."

"Pardon, my lady, but I should have supposed this to be the subject on which you would need no instruction."

"Perhaps I have had some success in the past at eliminating those obnoxious to me," said Hera. "But I seem to be losing my touch. Do you think I'm mellowing with age?"

"No, my queen, I do not. You seem to me as youthful, as energetic, as divinely vicious as ever. Perhaps even more so."

"You are too kind," murmured Hera. "The fact is that my worst enemy, the mortal I hate more than any other, more than

"Hercules is a special hero to children. . . .
We show him one . . . a little boy, wanting
to touch a weapon of the hero he adores."

any creature on earth, in the sea, or in your own smoky realm, continues to live and thrive despite my best efforts. I speak of Hercules, son of Zeus, by that cooing bitch, Alcmene, Lady of the Light Footsteps. Zeus has spawned swarms of children, as you know, and only two of them by me—and I hate and loathe and despise every one of them, of course. But worst of all, by far, do I abhor Hercules. For his mother was the most beautiful of my husband's paramours, and he is the strongest of Zeus's ill-gotten sons. Consequently, I decided to get him killed in the most painful way possible, and proceeded to involve him with monster after monster—all to no avail. He has overcome the Nemean Lion, the hundred-headed Hydra, and the three-bodied Geryon, fearsome creatures all, each of whom had devoured several generations of heroes. Now I'm at my wits' end and need your help, if you have any to give me."

"What we must do," said Hecate, "is find Hercules' weak point."

"Don't you think I've tried?" cried Hera. "I've confronted him with three of the most dreadful monsters ever hatched. While they were looking for his weak point, he slew them all."

"Allow me to differ, gracious lady. His adventure with the Hydra did reveal a weakness in him, perhaps a fatal one."

"I'm listening. . . ."

"It's not in the usual physical sense that he's vulnerable," said Hecate. "But he's cursed with a loving heart and an overheated imagination. He can be successfully attacked through those he cares for."

"Be specific."

"Hercules is a special hero to children. They dote on tales of his battles, follow him in hordes . . . and he is very fond of them."

"So?"

Hecate, Queen of the Harpies,
was the world's foremost expert on
various forms of vendetta and mayhem.

"So . . . this gives me an idea. As you know, he has never shot that arrow he dipped in Hydra blood. He's afraid the poison might spread. Well, we use this fear. We visit his sleep with a dream. We show him one of these children, a little boy, wanting to touch a weapon of the hero he adores. The boy rummages through Hercules' quiver and scratches his finger on an arrow— the poison arrow! The boy froths at the mouth, stiffens, dies. Hercules, knotted in this horrid nightmare, will view it not as a simple sleep vapor but as a prophetic vision, a solemn warning from on high. And once we hook him on this illusion, we'll know how to play him like a fish. We'll extract from him a penitential vow to go unarmed into his next adventure. And then we shall pit him, naked and weaponless, against a monster who has so far proved invincible, and whom I count as the most destructive force on earth."

"Who is this champion?"

"His name is Anteus, youngest son of Mother Earth and the Primal Snake, and the most fearsome of all that dreadful litter. He's a giant, presently king of Libya, and our current favorite down below. For the past few years, he has sent us more corpses than all other monsters combined."

"What makes him so invincible?" asked Hera.

"His size. His bloodlust. The fact that he has surrounded himself with a band of giants almost as fearsome as he is, and whom only he can control."

"I don't know . . ." murmured Hera. "When I think of Geryon and the Hydra and what Hercules did to them, I can't seem to put much confidence in ordinary giants."

"Anteus is no ordinary giant," said Hecate. "He is larger than the largest Titan, and of more than Titanic strength. He can kick over a fortified castle like an anthill and crush its defenders underfoot. Besides all this, he has a secret power. He is the favorite son of Mother Earth, and she has endowed him with a unique virtue. If ever thrown to earth, Anteus draws new strength from his mother. And no matter how grievously injured he has been, will arise whole, healed, unblemished, with strength restored. Doesn't he sound a little better to you, my lady?"

"Well, my dear," said Hera. "You are certainly eloquent on his behalf. Let's just hope for the best. Shall we start concocting that poison-arrow dream?"

6

Landfall in Libya

Thus it was that when Hercules crossed the Middle Sea to challenge Anteus, he carried no weapons. He did wear his lion skin—that hide he had taken from the Nemean Lion and which made a marvelous lightweight flexible armor—for it could turn any blade. As a helmet he wore the lion's skull. But horrified by his dream, keeping his own vow, he had left bow and arrows, spear, sword, and club behind.

He was rafting across the narrow arm of sea that divided the Iberian Peninsula from the northwestern spur of Africa ruled by Anteus. He had chosen a raft instead of a sailing vessel because this was the season when strong winds blew out of the south, and in those days sailboats could not tack; they could only run before the wind.

He had made his raft very simply, by lashing fallen trees together. Another tree trunk, which he had trimmed of branches, was his oar. The raft was unsinkable, but huge and clumsy—so heavy that twenty oarsmen would have been unable to manage it. But Hercules, using his single tree-trunk oar, made it skim over the water like a canoe.

Day and night he rowed. It was heavy work, moving the raft against headwinds, but he rowed without rest. Always before, he had gone joyously into battle, but this time for some reason he felt gloomy about the coming ordeal . . . and wanted to get it over with as quickly as possible. He was, however, to meet Anteus sooner than he wished.

Anteus enjoyed fishing, but the ordinary ways were far too tame for him. His idea of good sport was to wade out hip-deep—which meant about twenty feet of water—and there to hunt the man-eating sharks and giant octopi that lurked offshore. Before this, however, he would have provided himself with live bait, and his method of bait gathering was another of the royal techniques that terrified the Libyans.

He would appear in the courtyard at the morning lineup where prisoners were being thrown into the stewpot. Roaring, "You. . . you. . . you. . .," he would select six of them—eight if they were small—and, while they were still thanking him for their reprieve, would snatch them up in his huge paws and, two by two, knock their heads together. He did it gently, just enough to put them out; then he would stuff them in a sack and stride off toward the sea.

On this particular morning, the bait was more vigorous than usual. Some of the men in the sack came to and began to thrash about before Anteus reached the water. He raised his fist to smash at the restless bulge, but then thought: "The livelier they are the more they'll splash in the water. The more they splash the sooner they'll draw the sharks. . . ." So he simply shifted the sack on his shoulder and strode on.

He crossed the narrow beach and waded into the surf. The sea was rougher than usual. The south wind was behind him, blowing against the incoming tide, driving the breakers back on each other. Anteus frowned. Turbulent water meant that swimmers would be harder for the sharks to see. He would have to wait patiently in the water, or speed things up by spilling some blood. And Anteus had little patience.

When he was out far enough, he reached into the sack and pulled out one of the men, who screamed and struggled but was as helpless as a frog in the hands of a cruel boy. Anteus pinched his ear between thumb and forefinger and simply tore it off. He held the shrieking man upside down so that he could bleed into the water. Then, when the blood was spreading nicely, he tossed the man into the sea, and watched him as he began to swim frantically toward shore. Too late! A triangular black fin was cutting through the water toward him.

Anteus heard him utter a louder shriek, then disappear. But the giant made no move to catch this shark, for now there would be more blood upon the waters, attracting other sharks. Sure enough, he saw several fins slicing the tide toward the bloody foam. He ripped open the sack and spilled the other bait-men into the water, and grinned as he watched the fins coming closer.

For all Hercules' unique strength, rowing the heavy raft against the wind had almost drained him of energy, and he was very happy to be making landfall at last. But his happiness vanished as he heard whimpering and thin screams, and saw that the breakers were wearing manes of bloody spume.

Looking ahead, he saw an even worse sight. The biggest manlike creature he had ever met was standing waist-deep in water, scooping up sharks. He watched in disbelief. The giant, holding a great fish by the tail, snapped it in the air with such force that it became a blur. Hercules heard a loud cracking sound and realized that it was the shark's back snapping. The giant whirled and flung the dead fish toward shore. It sailed through the air and landed on the beach.

When the giant turned and saw Hercules, he dipped into the water and pulled out another shark and an enormous octopus. In the same motion, he threw them at Hercules.

There were some Titans and a few monsters and a giant or two who were stronger than Hercules, but none of them had reflexes so finely honed; none of them, in other words, could move as fast.

Now, when Anteus hurled shark and octopus at him, he swept the tree trunk that was his oar out of the water and swung it, smashing its base against the very center of the octopus's circular body, which was its head. It fell to the raft, stunned, and Hercules fell on top of it. The flung shark sailed over his head and landed in the water on the other side of the raft, and immediately breached, lunging toward Hercules.

The giant . . . dipped into the water and pulled out . . . an enormous octopus.

But he had snatched the stunned octopus from the deck of the raft and was using it as a shield, so that when the shark struck, its jaws closed on the great squid. Moving with magical celerity, Hercules began to knot the eight rubbery arms around the raging fish. Before Anteus had time to understand what was happening, Hercules tethered shark and octopus to each other and hurled them back at the giant . . . who lifted one huge paw and batted the fishy mass into the water.

"Greetings, stranger," he bellowed. "I see you're a man of meat, as we say here in Libya. And I offer you fine sport if you wish to come ashore and do a bit of real fighting."

"I accept your gracious invitation," called Hercules. "I do wish to come ashore. Your name is Anteus, is it not?"

"It is."

"King of Libya?"

"That's who I am."

"Well, I have come to fight you."

"As I mentioned," said Anteus. "I think we can provide you with some sport in that direction."

"But can we do it tomorrow?" asked Hercules. "I usually try to get down to these things immediately, but I find myself somewhat fatigued from my journey, and would be grateful for a night's rest before we meet."

"Do you expect to fight *me* tomorrow?"

"Yes, Your Majesty, if you don't mind waiting."

"You'll have to straighten out your thinking, little fellow. You don't start with me. I'm the champion. You'll have to work up to me."

"In all modesty, sir, I've done a few things myself. In the past year or so, I have defeated the Nemean Lion, the Hydra, and three-bodied Geryon."

"Yes, yes . . . enough for a nice little local reputation, no doubt, but a couple of moth-eaten monsters and a triple freak are not sufficient basis for challenging an Anteus. There are three of my helpers you'll have to defeat before I consent to meet you in single combat."

"All at once or one at a time?"

"One at a time, my friend. And you'll be in trouble enough, that way. You'll first meet my bowman, Gobi, and fight with bow and arrow. Should you, by chance, survive that match, you shall go against Mordo and fight with club or fist, as you prefer. If, by some incredible twist of luck, you emerge alive from that encounter, you shall be entitled to meet Kell, and duel with sword, spear, or battle-axe—anything with a sharp point or cutting edge. And if, miracle of miracles, you are still alive and intact after fighting Gobi, Mordo, and Kell, why then, little man, you shall have the honor of combating Anteus."

"Sounds interesting," said Hercules. "I am quite willing to go through all these preliminaries, if you wish, but I have one condition."

"Condition? Ha ha . . . I knew you'd try to back out of it."

"My condition, sir, is that I be permitted to go in unarmed against your archer, cudgeller, and man of blades."

"Unarmed?"

"Weaponless, yes. I have so vowed."

"Are you mad?"

"No, Your Majesty, quite sane. And very eager to commence hostilities."

"Greetings, stranger. . . . I offer
you fine sport if you wish to
come ashore and do a bit
of real fighting."

"Well, perhaps you're not so mad, after all. Go in weaponless, and you'll last about five seconds against Gobi . . . and be spared other suffering."

"Be that as it may," said Hercules. "I should be grateful for a night's rest before meeting the first of your henchmen."

"You shall have luxury accommodations," laughed Anteus. "Pray, come ashore."

7

Gobi

lthough Hercules had vowed to carry no weapon into this particular adventure, he did permit himself to wear his lion-skin armor when he faced Gobi. In fact, that impenetrable hide was the pivot of his battle plan. He intended to offer himself as a target and allow Gobi to shoot arrows at him, knowing that the shafts would be stopped by the lion skin. Then, when Gobi had emptied his quiver, Hercules planned to close with him and fight hand to hand.

But Anteus was wise in the ways of battle. When he saw Hercules clad in lion skin, he immediately knew what to do. He announced that the fight would be delayed, not held that morning, but at two hours past noon.

Hercules didn't realize the meaning of this until he had taken his position in the field and was waiting for Gobi to draw his bow. Peering through the eyeholes of the lion skull, he saw that Gobi was moving very deliberately—restringing his bow, taking one arrow from his quiver and studying it; then sliding it back and selecting another. Several minutes had passed and the archer had shot no arrow. Finally, he notched one, drew the great mam-

moth-tusk bow almost double, and let fly. The shaft whizzed through the air and struck the lion skin where it covered Hercules' chest. The arrow could not pierce the hide but it struck with great force. Hercules staggered. Looking down, he saw that the arrow lay on the ground; its point was broken off.

He looked toward Gobi again. The giant bowman had not pulled a second arrow, but was lounging there, smiling. Hercules couldn't understand it. Then, suddenly, he did. He realized that it had grown unbearably hot inside the heavy lion skin. This was the hottest hour of the day in the hottest month of the African summer. The sky was cloudless. The sun was a white-hot ball hanging right over his head. He was basting in his own sweat, and realized that Gobi meant to loiter there, wasting no arrows, but waiting for him to get so hot that he would have to strip off the lion skin and stand naked and unarmed before the deadly shafts.

Even as he was estimating the cost, he was shedding his lion skin. Every pore of his body rejoiced as the air touched his na-

46 *Hercules had vowed to carry no weapon into this particular adventure . . .*

kedness. But he didn't have much time to rejoice; an arrow was speeding toward him.

One of the secrets of Hercules' magical speed was that his mind did not direct his muscles; he thought *with* his body. Now, as the arrow sheared the golden air with such speed that its tail-feathers smoked, Hercules moved—as naturally and instinctively as a bird leaving a bough or a cat hooking its paw at a butterfly. He swerved, and the arrow that was going straight for his belly button just missed him; before it could pass, his hand shot out and grabbed it.

We know that Gobi's arrows were as big as ordinary spears. And Hercules, hefting the shaft, felt it as a well-balanced javelin. His conscience spoke:

"May I use this? Is it not a weapon? Am I breaking my vow? It's not *my* weapon, it's *his*. Does that make a difference?"

All this flashed through his mind more swiftly than a lizard flicking its tongue at a fly. But still too slowly. For Gobi had notched another arrow.

Without further thought Hercules flung his arrow like a javelin, but in a last scruple changed his aim so that he would strike not the archer but the bow. The arrow hurled by Hercules did strike the ivory bow, knocking it out of Gobi's hand.

Archers know that the least tremor in the fingers holding the bow or notching arrow to bowstring means a much larger difference when the arrow hits. So that a bowman trains himself to be very cool under stress. And Gobi could stand in the field, aiming his deadly bolts, stand solidly as a tree stump as enemy spears fell about him and chariots hurtled toward him.

Never before, however, had one of his arrows been caught in flight and used against him. Never before had he had the bow knocked out of his hand. And now, his coolness deserted him. He seized one of his arrows and, holding it before him like a lance, charged toward Hercules.

Hercules saw the huge figure hurtling toward him. He flexed his knees slightly, hunched his shoulders, poised his arms.

*The arrow sheared the golden air with
such speed that its tailfeathers smoked . . .*

A *cubit* was an ancient Greek measurement based on the average length of a full-grown man's forearm measured from elbow to wrist—or about eighteen of our inches. And Hercules was said to have been about six cubits in height, or nine feet tall. A giant, by our standards, or any mortal standard. But a real giant of the monster breed was about twenty feet tall and weighed in at half a ton, all muscle.

The giants belonging to Anteus's band were even larger, and the three he had chosen as his Royal Escort were the largest of all, reaching almost to Anteus's shoulder.

So that Hercules, big as he was, seemed like a child facing a raging adult as Gobi rushed across the field toward him. He

48

stood his ground, waiting. He had doffed the lion skin but still wore the lion-skull helmet. And when the javelin point reached him, he leaned forward, gauging the angle so that the arrow-lance did not hit the helmet squarely, but skidded off. Nevertheless, the glancing blow was enough to knock him off his feet, something which rarely occurred.

Gobi stood above him, grinning, and drove the lance down, aiming at Hercules' midriff, trying to pin him to the ground like an insect on a specimen board.

Hercules, lying flat, whisked away just in time, feeling the arrow graze his side as it buried itself in the ground. Gobi had struck with such force that the shaft had buried itself to half its length, and the giant had to jerk hard to pull it free, giving Hercules enough time to regain his feet.

Gobi raised his lance and jabbed again. But Hercules was not there. He had leaped high, high enough to bring his head level with Gobi's. And Hercules' head, it will be remembered, wore the lion-skull helmet. Hercules arched in the air, whipping his head forward with all the tensile strength of his neck, all the shocking force of the writhing muscles in his back and shoulders.

Lion skull struck giant skull, and that of the Nemean Lion was harder. Gobi's head cracked, spilling a gravy of pink-gray brains. He was dead when he hit the ground.

8

Mordo and Kell

nteus did not mourn the loss of Gobi. "Any giant who can get himself killed by an unarmed mortal is no giant I want around," he said. "Gobi's as well off dead as far as I'm concerned."

He was talking to Mordo. The gigantic, black-pelted bear-like cudgeller was leaning on his club, listening—grunting in agreement once in a while. Mordo spoke mostly in grunts.

"How about you now?" Anteus went on; "Did you learn anything from watching that poor excuse for a fight?"

"What I learned," said Mordo, "is that it won't be any use to hit him on the head while he's wearing that lion helmet. I'll just break my club."

"Poor thinking," said Anteus. "If you hit him hard enough, you'll ruin *his* head inside that helmet. Hit him, hit him! Break your damned club; you have plenty. But when you're through breaking clubs, your man's head should be a mush of blood and bone."

"Sounds good. I'll do it," grunted Mordo. "And I'm ready for him if he tries that jumping butting trick on me. I won't hold

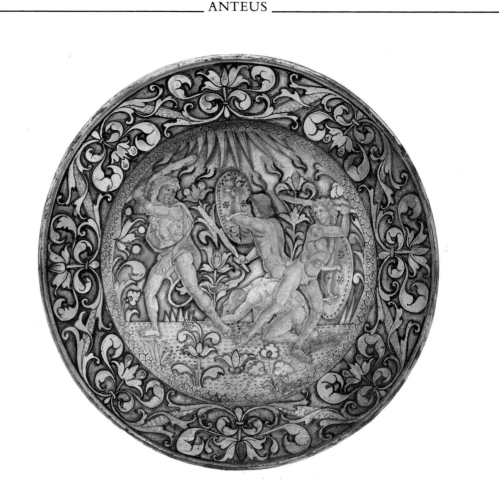

*Anyone stepping outside the circle
would be declared the loser . . .*

still for it like Gobi. I'll swat him in midair. Squash him like a
bug. I hope he tries it."

"Go in there and take him," said Anteus. "He seems to be
ready."

Mordo and Hercules faced each other in a tight ring of rocks
on a grassy plain. Anyone stepping outside the circle would be
declared the loser—the penalty for loss being immediate entry
into the stewpot. This rule was designed to keep the opponents
within arms' reach of each other, and served to favor the bigger,
slower Mordo, for it meant that Hercules could not use his speed.

But Anteus was making the rules, and Hercules did not really expect fair play.

Now, the young man knew that all the giants had watched him defeat Gobi and were very much aware that the lion-skull helmet could ward off any blow. So he expected Mordo to strike not downward at his head, but to sweep his club laterally in a blow designed to smash pelvis, rib cage, and chestbone, leaving him broken and helpless before Mordo, who could then, at his leisure, pound him to a bloody paste. And when the giant raised his cudgel high, clutching it in both hands, and started a downward smash, Hercules thought it was a feint—that Mordo would switch direction in midair, striking sideways at his torso.

But Mordo did not change direction. He continued the downward blow, smashing the enormous bludgeon down onto the lion-skull helmet. It was a terrible blow. Murderous. Mordo had practiced it on tree stumps, and was able to drive a massive oak stump into the ground as if it were a tent stake. So Hercules was quite unprepared for this dreadful blow to the head. The lion helmet held; the club shattered. But Hercules felt the column of his neck compressing; felt pain clamp his throat and claw down inside his chest. He felt himself suffocating; he couldn't breathe.

Nor could he think clearly. His head was ringing like a gong. Worst of all was the pain in his own skullbone. It was as if Hephaestus himself had laid his head on an anvil and was pounding it with his great iron mallet. He realized that while Mordo's blow had not broken his helmet, it had crushed it somewhat, tightening it around his temples, and causing this excruciating pain.

He reached up and yanked the helmet off, almost tearing away his ears in the process. Mordo watched, grinning, as Hercules staggered and reached up to pull off his helmet. Anteus had assured him that Hercules' head would be reduced to a paste of blood and bone, and he expected to see a gratifying gory hash when the helmet came off.

Now Mordo had always believed every word his chief said. And he was amazed to see his enemy's head emerge intact. His eyes were a bit unfocused and his face twisted in an effort to show no pain, but the head itself was definitely unbroken. And Mordo's club had shattered itself upon the helmet. His only weapons now were his fists. The prospect did not dismay him. He really preferred fists to clubs. He took a huge relish in using them. When he clenched his brutal hands and swung his enormous arms he was actually using two of the most dangerous kind of bone-studded cudgels, traveling faster and transmitting more sensation than any club. There was nothing he enjoyed more than driving those knuckles into an opponent's body, feeling bones crack, feeling the taut flesh grow slippery with blood.

Mordo swung his right arm. His fist, big as a cabbage, hard as a rock, arched toward Hercules' face. But that face was no longer there. The young man moved his head just enough to let the fist whiz past. Then he fell, as if knocked over by the wind of the passing fist. Mordo, reacting swiftly, did not realize that Hercules had fallen on purpose. He loomed over his sprawling foe and lifted his great foot, which was almost half the length of Hercules' body. His intention was to stomp that body to a bloody gruel.

But that was why Hercules had fallen—to get Mordo to do exactly what he was doing. Hercules' hand shot out, grasped Mordo's other ankle. Rising suddenly, he yanked the ankle with all his might, pulling the great stanchion of leg from under the giant. Mordo fell like a tree.

He started to scramble up. When Mordo had arisen to his knees, his face was level with Hercules'. Pivoting upon his ankles, the young man swung his own fist, striking Mordo full upon the throat, shattering his windpipe. The giant uttered a hoarse gurgling sound. His huge face went purple. His eyes bulged. Swaying upon his knees, he choked to death before the astounded gaze of Anteus and the other giants who had gathered to watch the fight.

Hercules was allowed no time to exult in his victory. For Kell attacked immediately. The head of his battle-axe was the blade of a massive ploughshare, honed to a razor edge. Its haft was the mast of a Cretan war-vessel, captured by the giants off the Libyan coast. This battle-axe, wielded by the gigantic butcher, was the biggest and heaviest in the entire world.

Its blade glittered now in the afternoon sun as Kell came rushing over the plain to attack Hercules. It was a wide grassy plain, a great meadow. But some miles off, Hercules had ob-

Hercules yanked the ankle with all
his might. . . . Mordo fell like a tree.

The giant had raised his axe high and
began a downward blow . . .

served, was a stand of oak marking the edge of a forest. The young man realized that it would be fatal to fight Kell in the open; that enormous whirling blade would joint him like a plucked chicken in the hands of a kitchen slave. He turned from his enemy and began to run.

He darted across the plain, and Kell followed. Now, Hercules could run faster than any mortal, but, as noted, giants can cover an inhuman amount of ground in a single stride. Kell, however, was slowed somewhat by the weight of the axe he was carrying and, fast as he was going, could not quite catch up to Hercules.

The giant was amazed to see his enemy stop when he reached the oak grove. "Guess he's winded," thought Kell. Roaring like an entire pride of lions, he charged into the grove, swinging his axe.

Hercules dodged behind a tree. Axe blade met tree trunk, and sheared the enormous bole at its base. Hercules had to leap thirty feet from a standing position to escape the crashing boughs. He was in mortal peril, he knew. That huge sharp axe thirsted for his blood, and there seemed no way to defend against it.

This time he chose a straight half-grown tree to shelter behind. Kell whirled his axe, slashing at the tree. The blade passed through the trunk as if it were a celery stalk. The tree actually rose in the air before it began to fall. Hercules caught it as it fell.

"I vowed to fight without weapons," he thought. "And I've tried, I've tried. Can I help it if the enemy insists on arming me?"

There was no more time to examine his conscience. The giant had raised his axe high and begun a downward blow that would divide Hercules from pate to heel. He jumped on a stump, swinging his tree trunk, swinging it level to the ground in a vicious sideways swipe that caught Kell in the side and smashed his rib cage. These ribs were as tough and springy as the hoops of a great wine keg. When they were smashed by Hercules' club, their splinters became a dozen knives ripping into the giant's lungs.

Kell sank to his knees, gasping and coughing. A red froth bubbled from his mouth. He fell among the fallen branches and lay still.

Standing among his courtiers, Anteus felt himself swelling with fury. This puny little stranger had stripped him of his Royal

Escort—killed his three best fighters and most loyal counsellors, all in one afternoon.

He would not wait for a formal match, he decided. He would go out there right now, catch the miserable cur in the very flush of his triumph—yes, slowly, deliberately, luxuriously, would clamp his gigantic hands about Hercules' torso the way a murderer of normal size would seize a victim by the neck and choke him. So he would take Hercules' body in his two hands and slowly, slowly, close them, squeezing so hard that the man's guts would ooze out of his mouth.

He started toward Hercules but caught himself in mid-stride. "Poor idea," he thought. "The sun's sinking; it's almost dark." And, light or dark, there was no one there except his own court to observe what he meant to do to Hercules. That wasn't enough. For already, no doubt, the news of the stranger's victories would have spread abroad. People would be talking about him. Rejoicing, jeering. No! He needed an audience to watch him execute this loathsome Hercules. An immense throng. He would bring all Libya to watch, and to learn again the awful power of their king.

Thereupon, he summoned Hercules, and boomed out for all to hear: "Congratulations, little Theban. You have performed well in your preliminary matches, and have earned the right to meet the champion, namely me. We shall fight tomorrow. In the meantime, eat, drink, rest yourself. Dinner tonight will be the last one you'll ever eat, no doubt. Is there any dish you'd particularly like?"

"I thank you for your courtesy, my host," replied Hercules. "And I'll eat anything but your stew."

Anteus had thought it best to conceal his feelings, but they boiled over again that night when he prowled the countryside, too angry to sleep. For now, once again, the faint mocking strains of the old song were borne upon the wind, but with its lines slightly changed:

"Gobi, Mordo, Kell . . .
Bowman, Banger, Butcher,
They served the tyrant well . . .
But now they're sent below,
to wait for him in hell . . ."

Anteus managed to hunt down some of the singers. He bore them to the courtyard of his castle and threw them into the stewpot. Their screams lulled him for a little while. Still, the night seemed very long. Nor would morning bring relief. It would take several hours, he knew, to assemble a great crowd to view the humiliation and destruction of Hercules.

9

A Gift of Fire

To understand what happened next in the strange conflict between the young hero, Hercules, and the monstrous earth-giant, Anteus, we must go back toward the first days when Prometheus was trying to befriend the newly created race called man. The Titan looked down from heaven one day and didn't like what he saw.

Men and women crouched in dark caves, cold, almost naked. They used tools chipped out of stone and ate their meat raw. They were dulled, brutish, speaking to each other in grunts. Prometheus went to Zeus, and said:

"Why, oh Thunderer, do you keep the race of man in ignorance and darkness?"

"What you call ignorance is innocence," said Zeus. "What you call darkness is the shadow of my decree. Man is happy now and will remain happy until someone tells him he is unhappy. Do not meddle further with my designs."

"I know that everything you do is wise," said Prometheus. "Enlighten me with your wisdom. Tell me why you refuse humankind the gift of fire?"

"Because hidden in this race is a pride that can destroy us. Give him the great servant called fire and he will try to make himself as powerful as the gods. Why, he would storm Olympus. Go now, and trouble me no further."

But Prometheus was not satisfied. The next morning he stood tiptoe on a mountaintop and stole some fire from the sunrise. He hid the spark in a hollow reed, then went down to earth. And went from cave to cave where men and women crouched, shivering, eating their meat raw.

Zeus, looking down later, could not believe what he was seeing. Everything was changed. Man had come out of his cave. Zeus saw huts, farmhouses, walled towns, a castle. He saw people cooking their food, carrying torches to light their way at night. Forges blazed; smiths were beating out ploughs, keels, swords, spears. Men were raising white wings of sails and daring to use the fury of the wind for their passages. They were wearing helmets, riding chariots into battle like the gods themselves.

Zeus was furious. He knew whom to blame. He ordered Prometheus seized and bound to a mountain peak in a place where it always snows and where the wind howls ceaselessly. There the friend of man was sentenced to spend eternity, chained to a crag, two vultures hovering about him, tearing at his belly and eating his liver. He was immortal and could not die, but he could suffer. And suffer he did through long centuries for giving mankind the gift of fire.

It was a curious thing, but the image of the tortured god had a way of dissolving into starlight—becoming a kind of dream-pollen carried by the night airs and blowing into the sleep of those who suffered: orphans, widows, widowers, those otherwise bereft or deserted, sick people, dying people, prisoners. A stormy blue light entered their sleep, bathing a mountain crag where was chained a Titan with a torn belly, whose entrails were being devoured by a pair of vultures. The wind shrieked in that dream, mingling with the screams of the raw-headed birds, but the Titan uttered no sound.

And the look of utter stubborn courage on his face above the torn body acted to calm the dreamers—made them meet their own torments with a deeper acceptance, and slip into a deeper sleep.

Weary Hercules was having a hard time trying to sleep under an African sky too strange to offer repose. Night here was no absence of light but the presence of living darkness. It pressed on him with weird power. The stars were too big; they were daubs of crude light pinned on a great blowing sky. The wind strengthened. A black wind. It blew out the stars. Blackness flowed into his head. He felt he might sleep.

The hot blackness went away. He was being bathed in another light—a blue stormy light. He saw a mountain peak;

Everything was changed. . . . Men were wearing helmets,
riding chariots into battle like the gods themselves.

*The friend of man was sentenced to spend
eternity chained to a crag, two vultures
hovering about him, tearing at his belly.*

snow lurked upon it. Not snow, but the flowing white hair and white beard of an enormous old man. Too big for a man. A Titan, bound to the crag. Birds dived at him; their screams mingled with the wind. And now the Titan's voice mixed with wind and bird-cry:

"Hercules . . . Hercules."

"I am here," he heard himself answer. "But not for long."

"You sound discouraged."

"I don't understand it," muttered Hercules. "I'm not usually low spirited before a fight. I'm usually happy, excited, full of confidence. But now, I'm full of foreboding."

"That's a good way to defeat yourself."

"I know. I know. I'm ashamed of myself."

"That's unprofitable too," said the Titan. And, although he seemed to be speaking softly, his voice rose effortlessly over wind-howl and bird-shriek. "I mean to help you, you know."

"Do you?" said Hercules. "You look like you could use some help yourself."

"Yes, and you are the one who shall save me from my ordeal if I succeed in saving your life tomorrow."

"Sounds eminently fair," said Hercules. "I am all attention, venerable sir."

"Listen closely, lad. A bird will come to you at dawn. She will fly straight out of the sunrise so that she will seem to be all ablaze. And, indeed, this singular bird abides in the core of flame and is unconsumed . . . but resurrects herself from the ashes. Her name is Phoenix. I know her ways because I am familiar with fire. The Phoenix will fly to you. You will welcome her and pluck one of her feathers—the single blue feather that grows among the red feathers of her breast. That magic plume cools the heat of the hottest flame and may save your life tomorrow."

"A blue feather from her breast . . . yes . . ."

"My time is up. Farewell. And blessings of the Phoenix be upon you."

The blue-white cone of light faded. The African night pressed about Hercules again. He entered the hot blackness. He slept. And when the bird came flying out of the kindling sky at dawn, its feathers dyed with the colors of sunrise, he hardly knew whether he was awake or dreaming. But he pulled the blue feather from the blazing red chest of the gorgeous bird, as the Titan had instructed.

10

Hero Meets Monster

The giant, Anteus, liked everything about him to be big. When he performed, meaning when he fought in public, he ordered huge crowds to be assembled. And, because a system of compulsory attendance always guarantees a big audience, Anteus knew that the huge amphitheater would be filled upon this day, and that if he killed Hercules by early afternoon, as he intended, all Libya would know about it by nightfall.

They were to fight in a natural amphitheater where low hills cupped a flat stretch of meadow. Vast throngs could be seated on the slopes, and the largest of all had been assembled to watch Hercules fight Anteus. It wasn't the usual sullen mob, but one that seemed alive with joy and hope. For, although they had been rousted out of their homes by the Royal Guard and herded like cattle to the amphitheater, nevertheless they were happy to be there. For word had spread. This stranger who had dared to challenge Anteus had come on a raft and seemed indeed to be the very embodiment of the ancient prophecy, which told the Libyans that a hero one day would come from the sea to deliver them from the tyrant. If the rumors were true, this had to be the Promised One. For it was said that he, alone and weaponless, had slain Gobi, Mordo, and Kell, all in a single afternoon.

So they were abrim with hope before the fight began. But their hope changed to shocked dismay when they saw Hercules. Why, the whole thing must be a lie! This youth down there was big for a mortal, but surely not big enough to have killed the Bowman, the Banger, and the Butcher. He barely reached to Anteus's kneecap.

Hercules was keenly attuned to the mood swing of the crowd. He had seen them literally steaming with hope on their hot hillsides, and he understood their collective moan when they had identified him as the one who would fight Anteus. But the young man drove that thought from his head; he had more important things to think about.

Anteus had come into the arena, had stripped and was being oiled by slaves. To reach his great height, they had to lean ladders against him and toil up the rungs with sponges and buckets of oil until they reached the wide plateau of his shoulders and the enormous keg of his chest—then they would ply their sponges, swabbing him with oil.

Hercules down below studied the giant as he was being groomed. He was looking for a vulnerable spot. But as he examined the thewed pillars of those legs, the bulging torso, the enormous cabled arms, the keg of a chest—and his head, which seemed to have been rough-hewn out of rock—as Hercules studied Anteus, he simply did not know where to attack.

But attack he must. He had to strike first. He simply could not wait for the giant to go into action. He tried to remember all he had learned about how the body was built. His gaze was drawn to the giant's head. Somewhere there. But where? What could any fist do against that rocky crag of head? His eyes were so deeply socketed between beetling brow and jutting cheekbone that no one could possibly gouge them. The most fragile spot of the head, Hercules knew, was the platelet of bone behind the ear. In mortal man, a sharp blow upon that mastoid bone would shatter it, driving splinters into the brain, causing instant death. And even if all the giant's bones were armor-plate thick compared to a man's, still, in proportion, that bone behind the ear would be the most fragile. It was worth a try, anyway. It was his only chance. But how to reach it?

Now in a flash, he began to think with his body. Idea became action. He edged into the stream of slaves filing toward the ladder, pushed one out of line—gently, so as not to hurt him—seized bucket and sponge, and raced up the rungs of the ladder that was leaning against Anteus. No one noticed. He scuttled up like a squirrel. He stepped onto Anteus's shoulder, trying not to slip on the oily slope.

He eased himself toward the back of the shoulder, grasped the giant's ear, yanked at it, turning the head a bit, then swung his fist so fast that his arm was a golden blur in the sunlight. He felt a sharp pain in his knuckles as they broke bone, almost breaking themselves.

Ladders tumbled, buckets flew as the giant swayed. Slaves slid off him and fell to the ground. And Anteus himself, after reeling a moment, collapsed like a stone tower in an earthquake.

Hercules, feeling the giant beginning to fall, had slid down the oiled arm and dropped safely to the ground. He stood there on the grass gazing down at the vast empty-looking face of his enemy. It was ashy, that face. Life seemed to have fled. He had no way of knowing about the malign magic that invested Anteus; no way of knowing that the giant, born of Mother Earth, was always renewed by contact with his mother.

But Hercules was to learn his lesson very painfully. He started back in horror as he saw the great eyelids snap open, saw those deeply socketed eyes blazing with furious energy. Before he could flee, a great arm raised itself. A hand bigger than a grappling hook caught him by the middle and lifted him high. Hercules hung there, clenched in that hand, as Anteus rose to his full height.

Standing there in the sunny arena, the giant pivoted slowly, holding Hercules high for all to see. Then, slowly, he lowered Hercules. Took him in both hands. Held him almost tenderly, it

*Ladders tumbled, buckets flew as the giant
swayed. Slaves slid off him and fell to the ground.*

seemed, as a boy might hold a puppy. He spoke softly, just loud
enough for Hercules to hear:

"How shall I do it, little one? Shall I squeeze you to a pulp?
Or shall I twist you in my two hands—twist and twist until your
spine is torn away from your pelvis and you are in two pieces,
one for each hand? Which, eh? . . . Well, it's a pleasant choice I
have to make. They're both slow deaths, squeezing and twisting,
but still not quite slow enough. The pain simply won't last as
long as I should like it to. I cannot forget the way you killed my
three best servants. Oh, you'll have to pay for that, pay and pay.
Squeezing is much too easy a death. Twisting too. Nor are those
methods quite dramatic enough—for my hands will mask your

sufferings, muffle your screams. People won't really know what's happening to you. Or, at least, they'll miss the full glory of it. No! I mean to do something showy. I'm going to take you these few miles to the stewpot, and the crowd will follow us. We'll be a regular procession. And when we reach the pot I'll add you to the stew with full honors. When you're done, I'll order a great holiday feast. I'll make them swallow every last greasy drop; I'll choke them on their own hopes."

He lifted Hercules high again. His voice thundered at the great throng.

"Follow me, all of you! Follow me to the courtyard and see what happens to one who offends your king. Come, come . . . up and away! Who lingers, dies."

He marched out of the arena and toward the castle. The people came slowly off the slopes and followed him in a mournful procession.

Now, when terribly threatened—something that happened often—Hercules conducted himself in heroic fashion. He deliberately shut off a useless part of his mind. He wasted no time regretting any mistakes he might have made, nor did he allow himself to anticipate anything bad that might happen. He forced himself to live one second at a time, tuning his body to respond instantly to any opportunity for survival.

So he lay now very quietly in the giant's hands. He knew that the slightest movement might arouse a reflex of brutality in those hands and make them move of themselves, no matter what Anteus intended. He lay there, hardly daring to breathe, just taking tiny sips of air. He had rejoiced when the giant had decided to leave the arena and take him to the castle. He did not allow himself to think of the stewpot; time enough for that when it happened. All he permitted himself to think was that the giant's intention gave him a little more time to live.

Still the enormous hands clamped him, not squeezing, causing him no pain, but holding him too tightly for him to wriggle

*The people came slowly off the slopes and
followed the giant in a mournful procession.*

free. All he could do was wait. But when he reached the castle
he shuddered despite himself. It was a windless day and the steam
of the stew hung heavy over the courtyard. He felt himself gag-
ging in the sweetish putrefying stench of boiled human flesh.

Now, he was rising into the air again. Anteus was lifting
him over his head. The giant held him high for all to see. His
voice boomed:

"Oh, Libyans, I have invited you here today that you might
see what happens to one who dares challenge your king. This is
Hercules I hold here. Hercules of Thebes, who for all his insignificant size has proved himself in battle against very worthy foes.
Emboldened by his success with some local monsters, he came

to Libya to challenge me, Anteus. And, indeed, even here he managed to wreak a bit of mischief among my people. Observe him well, my friends, as he lies helpless in my hands. Look at him, this hero, harmless as a flayed rabbit in the hands of a hunter . . . fit only for the pot. Indeed, that is why I have brought him here: to add him to our royal stew."

Hercules felt the fingers shift on his body, and knew that the giant was about to throw him into the stewpot. He braced himself. His own fingers felt for the blue feather taken from the breast of the Phoenix. Prometheus had promised that this magic plume would protect him from heat. But would it protect him from drowning in the abominable stew? Or, if he did not drown, from suffocating in its stench?

Anteus suddenly drew Hercules toward his face as if he meant to eat him raw. The young man saw the great yolky eyes glaring at him, saw the teeth big as tombstones, and the huge meaty tongue behind them.

"No," grunted Anteus. "On second thought, you're too vile a creature for my stew. You might spoil the flavor. *Under* the pot is where you belong, in the cook-fire. Yes . . . roasting's just as slow as boiling, and just as painful."

Anteus lifted Hercules over his head again, roared, "Behold!" and hurled him into the very center of the wood fire that was blazing under the huge stewpot. Hercules landed in the heart

of the fire, and crouched there, clutching his Phoenix feather. Steam arose from him as fire touched his wet body. He welcomed the steam for it hid him from sight. And he didn't want Anteus to see him sitting amid flame in a magical sheath of coolness cast by the ice-blue plume.

Nevertheless, he felt the enchantment beginning to melt in the intense heat. He needed a more intense blueness, more whiteness, the more powerful magic of ancient wisdom. Perching there in the core of flame, he sent his thoughts halfway across the world to a mountain in the Caucasus where Prometheus lay

The young man saw the great yolky eyes . . . the teeth big as tombstones, and the huge meaty tongue behind them.

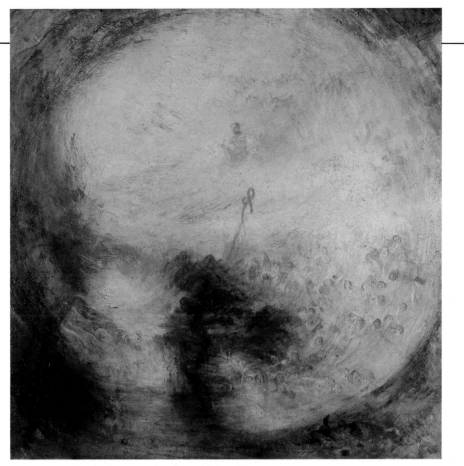

Perching there in the core of the flame,
Hercules sent his thoughts halfway across the world . . .

shackled. Once again he was fixed in a cone of stormy blue light. Once again, he saw snow in cracks of rock. And the sight of bloody-beaked birds tearing at the Titan's guts made his own pain seem insignificant. He heard the rich voice rising above the screaming of the birds and the howling of the wind:

"You are he."

"Who?" whispered Hercules.

"The Promised One. For the Libyans. For me."

"For you?"

"Even for me. In the watches of night, a voice has spoken with utter authority, saying, 'Whom the father torments, the son will save.' "

"What father? What son?"

"In time to come, son of Zeus, all shall be made clear. But for now, the now that must always come first, hearken to this: As your enemy, Anteus, the son of Earth, is restored by touching his mother, so shall you, Hercules, be restored by fire. I, the fire-giver, tell you so. The sacred flame shall heal you, restore you. In return, you shall deliver me one day. And now, arise. Go forth. Fight again."

Anteus approached the fire, waiting for the steam to lift, hoping to see his enemy charring as he sizzled in his own juices. The steam did lift. Something moved behind it. Anteus gaped in horror as Hercules hopped out of the fire. The young man was smiling. He seemed to gleam with health. His wounds were healed. He was uncharred, unscarred.

For the first time in his life, Anteus took a backward step in the presence of an enemy. But he was stupefied by shock. Then his fighting instincts took over. He stood where he was and considered what to do. One thing he knew: that when he caught that little rat again he wouldn't let him out of his hands until he was in many pieces.

Hercules did not wait for his enemy to move. Because all ways of fighting Anteus seemed equally impossible, Hercules did what he always did when he was in doubt: he charged. And the people who thronged the courtyard were amazed to see the man hurtling toward the giant.

Anteus stood waiting. Then he swung his leg in a terrible kick. Hercules glimpsed the foot coming toward him with enormous speed, and in full stride scooped up a paving stone, which he held before him. The giant's foot hit the stone. The small bones of the instep and ankle shattered like glass. It was agony. He hopped on his other foot. Hercules shoved his shoulder against that leg and pushed it out from under Anteus, who crashed to the ground.

The walls of the courtyard trembled as the giant fell full length, cracking his head on a flagstone. Hercules heard the dry sound of the head splitting. Heard the rattling gasp of his enemy's breath. Saw blood welling out of the split head and forming puddles on the stone. He stood over his enemy, watching him die.

He was astounded to see the blood stopping. To hear the hoarse gasping stop. He saw the giant's eyes flare with rage, saw the great biceps swell. Before he could dodge, Anteus reached out. His huge fingers caught Hercules by the throat and began to squeeze. The flagstones tilted; the sky darkened. Hercules tried to tear those strangling fingers from his throat. But in no fight he had ever fought with monsters of land and sea had he known a force to match that of Anteus—who, lounging on the ground, was easily choking him to death with one hand.

And as his sight faded, he heard again the voice of Prometheus saying: "He is born of Mother Earth. When he touches her, his strength is restored." And Hercules realized that he had repeated his first mistake—had laid his enemy in his mother's lap, and she had revived him, healed him, restored his strength.

This awful truth glimmered in his murky mind, but flared up brightly as truth does even when things look darkest. Again he heard the voice of Prometheus. "You shall be restored by fire, even as he is by earth." And the idea carried by these words cast a light that became power beyond the strength of muscles. He slashed the edge of his palm at Anteus's elbow, making the elbow crook, and loosening the grip on his throat. He moved closer to Anteus and wedged his hands underneath the giant.

Drawing enormous breath into his tortured lungs, he grasped Anteus about the waist and began to pull him off the ground. Anteus kicked and flailed and clung to the earth. His mother, Gaia, Mother Earth, knowing her favorite son in danger, put forth her magnetic strength—which is called gravity—trying to hug her son to her, to keep him safe.

Hercules couldn't pull him off the ground. And knew that if he didn't he was lost. He pulled with all his strength. Anteus clung to the earth—who hugged him close. "Fire-giver, help me

now," whispered Hercules. And with these words, he felt his veins begin to run with flame. He saw the suffering Titan whose gift had transformed humankind, lifting it out of brutish darkness into light—he felt that magic voltage enter every fiber of his body, filling him with a power that enabled him to tear the giant from the clutch of earth and lift him slowly toward the sky.

Holding Anteus away from earth, he saw the great cracked head begin to bleed again. Saw the light fade from his eyes. Felt the huge throbbing body go limp as a bladder. He kept holding the body even after he knew it was dead; he didn't dare let it touch earth again.

People were shouting now, roaring, shrieking with joy. He marched toward the stewpot and threw Anteus in. The body landed with a great splash. Hercules turned to the roaring crowd:

"He will feed you now whom you have fed so long."

People clustered about the pot. They lifted it from its hooks. They did not dip in. They refused to eat the stew. They wanted no part of Anteus, even dead. They bore the great cauldron to the beach and emptied it into the sea and watched the black fins cut through the water. Sharks prefer live meat, but Anteus was only recently dead, and very large; so they feasted happily as the people danced on the beach.

Another group of dancing, cheering youths bore Hercules on their shoulders. They carried him to the harbor where he had asked to go. There he borrowed a sailing vessel, for the south wind was still blowing, and his ship would be able to run before it all the way home. This pleased him; he felt too stiff to push a raft through the Middle Sea.

Acknowledgments

Letter Cap Illustrations by Hrana L. Janto

Opposite page 1, PANIC (COLOSSUS) by *Francisco Goya (1746–1828), oil on canvas (45 5/8 x 41 3/8")*
    Courtesy of The Prado, Madrid
        Photo: Scala/Art Resource, New York

Page 3, BUTCHER SHOP AT THE CORNER OF HUNGER AND HELL *(1985/86) by Emilio Cruz, oil on canvas (6 x 7')*
    Courtesy of the Artist and Anita Shapolsky Gallery, New York

Page 4, THE TEMPEST *by Alberto Savinio (1891–1952), oil on canvas*
    Courtesy of a private collection, Milan
        Photo: Scala/Art Resource, New York

Page 6, SHE SHALL BE CALLED WOMAN *by William Blake (1757–1827), pen and ink and watercolor, over light pencil indications, on paper (16 7/8 x 13 3/8"), signed (lower left corner) with monogram.*
    Courtesy of The Metropolitan Museum of Art, Rogers Fund, 1960 (06.1322.2)

Page 9, THE HOUSE OF DEATH *(ca. 1795) by William Blake, watercolor (17 x 21 1/8")*
    Courtesy of The Tate Gallery, London

Page 10, CONVOCATION OF THE GODS *by Giuseppe Maria Crespi (1665–1747), ceiling fresco*
    Courtesy of the Palazzo Pepoli, Bologna
        Photo: Scala/Art Resource, New York

Page 14, NEPTUNE AND DOLPHIN, *attributed to Gianlorenzo Bernini (1598–1680), bronze sculpture*
    Courtesy of the Galleria Borghese, Rome
        Photo: Scala/Art Resource, New York

Page 16, JONAH *by Albert Pinkham Ryder (1847–1917), oil on canvas (69 x 87 cm.)*
    Courtesy of The National Museum of American Art, Washington, D.C.
        Photo: Rosenthal/Art Resource, New York

Page 18, HEAD OF A WOMAN *by Pablo Picasso (1881–1973), linoleum cut, printed in black, dark brown, light brown and beige, Arches paper, edition of 50 (image 25 1/4 x 20 3/4")*
    Courtesy of The Metropolitan Museum of Art; The Mr. and Mrs. Charles Kramer Collection; Gift of Mr. and Mrs. Charles Kramer, 1979 (1979.620.53)

Page 21, NUDE WOMAN AT A SPRING *by Pablo Picasso, linoleum cut, printed in black, dark brown, light brown and beige, Arches paper, edition of 50 (image 20 3/4 x 25 1/8")*
> Courtesy of The Metropolitan Museum of Art; The Mr. and Mrs. Charles Kramer Collection; Gift of Mr. and Mrs. Charles Kramer, 1979 (1979.620.82)

Page 23, NUDE MALE KNEELING *by Michelangelo (1475–1564), charcoal on paper*
> Courtesy of Gabinetto Disegni, Florence
>> Photo: Scala/Art Resource, New York

Page 24, Detail from CHRIST CARRYING THE CROSS *by Hieronymus Bosch (1450–1516), oil on canvas*
> Courtesy of the Ghent Museum
>> Photo: Kavaler/Art Resource, New York

Page 28, HERCULES AND THE HYDRA *by Antonio Pollaiuolo (ca. 1431–1498), oil on canvas*
> Courtesy of the Uffizi Gallery, Florence
>> Photo: Scala/Art Resource, New York

Page 30, THE TOILETTE OF JUNO *by Andrea Appiani (1754–1817), oil on canvas*
> Courtesy of Pinacoteca Civica, Brescia
>> Photo: Scala/Art Resource, New York

Page 32, Detail from CONFIRMATION OF THE RULE *by Domenico Ghirlandaio (1449–1494), mural*
> Courtesy of The Palazzo Medici, Florence
>> Photo: Scala/Art Resource, New York

Page 33, HECATE, *detail from* JUPITER AND SEMELE *by Gustave Moreau (1826–1898), oil on canvas*
> Courtesy of Musée de Gustave Moreau, Paris
>> Photo: Giraudon, Paris

Page 36, SHIPPING OF WOOD BY SEA *(ca. 8th century B.C.), Assyrian stone relief*
> Courtesy of The Louvre, Paris
>> Photo: Giraudon/Art Resource, New York

Page 39, THE BOOK OF URIZEN *(1794) by William Blake, Plate 6:* URIZEN STRUGGLING IN THE WATERS OF MATERIALISM *(11 11/32 x 9 1/4")*
> Courtesy of The British Museum, London

Page 40, OCTOPUS VASE *(ca. 1500 B.C.), Minoan pottery*
> Courtesy of the National Museum, Athens
>> Photo: Jan Lukas/Art Resource, New York

Page 42, THE LAESTRYGONIANS PREPARING TO ATTACK ULYSSES *(late 1st century B.C.), Roman wall painting*
> Courtesy of The Museo Profano, The Vatican
>> Photo: Scala/Art Resource, New York

Page 44, RISING *by Adolph Gottlieb (1903–1974), oil on canvas (72 x 48")*
> Courtesy of The Rose Art Museum, Brandeis University, Waltham, Massachusetts
> Gervirtz-Mnuchin Purchase Fund
>> Photo: Muldoon Studio

Page 46, HERCULES, *detail from* PITTORE DI ATHENA *(ca. 450 B.C.), Greek vase*
> Courtesy of the National Museum, Athens
>> Photo: Nimatallah/Art Resource, New York

Page 48, BIRDS SWOOPING DOWN AND ARROWS *by Paul Klee (1879–1940), watercolor, transferred printing ink on gesso on paper (21 x 26 1/2 cm.)*
Courtesy of The Metropolitan Museum of Art; The Berggruen Klee Collection, 1984 (1984.315.14)

Page 50, Detail from A BRONZE DOOR *(11th century), Augsburg Cathedral, Germany*
Photo: Art Resource, New York

Page 52, HERCULES SLAYING GIANTS *(ca. 1510), Majolica ware plate (diameter 18 1/4")*
Courtesy of The Metropolitan Museum of Art; Robert Lehman Collection, 1975 (1975.1.1036)

Page 55, HERCULES AND CAUCUS *by Domenichino (1581–1641), oil on canvas*
Courtesy of The Louvre, Paris
Photo: Scala/Art Resource, New York

Page 56, Detail from THE MONTH OF DECEMBER *(14th century), mural by anonymous artist*
Courtesy of the Castello del Buonconsiglio, Trento
Photo: Scala/Art Resource, New York

Page 60, ANGEL OF THE REVELATION *by William Blake, watercolor with pen and ink on paper (15 7/16 x 10 1/4"), signed with monogram*
Courtesy of The Metropolitan Museum of Art; Rogers Fund, 1914 (14.81.1)

Page 63, ALLEGORY OF WAR *(1825) by Frantisek Tradlik, oil on canvas*
Courtesy of the National Gallery, Prague
Photo: Art Resource, New York

Page 64, PROMETHEUS *by Gustave Moreau, oil on canvas (80 3/4 x 48")*
Courtesy of Musée de Gustave Moreau, Paris
Photo: Giraudon/Art Resource, New York

Page 66, BURIAL OF THE SARDINE *(1793) by Francisco Goya, oil on wood (32 5/8 x 24 3/8")*
Courtesy of the Academia de San Fernando, Madrid
Photo: Scala/Art Resource, New York

Page 70, PREMONITION *(1986) by Ricardo Cinalli, pastel on tissue paper (86 x 112")*
Courtesy of the Vanderwoude Tananbaum Gallery, New York

Page 72–73, LA ROMERIA DI SAN ISIDRO *by Francisco Goya, oil on canvas*
Courtesy of The Prado, Madrid
Photo: Scala/Art Resource, New York

Page 74, Detail from THE TEMPTATION OF ST. ANTHONY *by Hieronymus Bosch, oil on canvas*
Courtesy of The Prado, Madrid
Photo: Art Resource, New York

Page 75, LIGHT AND COLOR (GOETHE'S THEORY)—THE MORNING AFTER THE DELUGE *by Joseph Mallord William Turner (1775–1851), oil on canvas (31 x 31")*
Courtesy of the Tate Gallery, London
Photo: The Bridgeman Art Library, London

Page 78, HERCULES AND ANTAEUS *by Antonio Pollaiuolo, oil on canvas*
Courtesy of the Uffizi Gallery, Florence
Photo: Scala/Art Resource, New York

BOOKS BY BERNARD EVSLIN

Merchants of Venus
Heroes, Gods and Monsters of the Greek Myths
Greeks Bearing Gifts: The Epics of Achilles and Ulysses
The Dolphin Rider
Gods, Demigods and Demons
The Green Hero
Heraclea
Signs & Wonders: Tales of the Old Testament
Hercules
Jason and the Argonauts